ILLUSTRATED BY GUY FIELD

WRITTEN BY GARY PANTON
AND JOCELYN NORBURY

EDITED BY JOCELYN NORBURY
DESIGNED BY KIM HANKINSON
COVER DESIGN BY JOHN BIGWOOD
CONSULTANCY BY SUSIE HODGE

First published in Great Britain in 2020 by LOM ART, an imprint of
Michael O'Mara Books Limited, 9 Lion Yard, Tremadoc Road, London SW4 7NQ

W www.mombooks.com/lom
f Michael O'Mara Books
@OMaraBooks
@lomartbooks

A CIP catalogue record for this book is available from the British Library.

ISBN: 978-1-912785-17-9

10 9 8 7 6 5 4 3 2 1

Printed in China

CONTENTS

"IDEAS
ALONE CAN
BE WORKS
OF ART."

Sol LeWitt

INTRODUCTION

"I could have done that!" is a cliché that can be heard echoing around galleries the world over. You may even have said it yourself. And it's true that many famous pieces of art look as though they required little skill, time or attention to detail. So why ARE they hanging on gallery walls?

For a start, there's a lot we can learn from even the most simple pieces, not least that there's far more to them than the finished product. The art featured in this book is important not just for how it looks, but for what it represents. In some cases, the artist might have worked in a variety of styles throughout their careers, responding to multiple influences and reference points.

In this book you'll find information about each artist, their style and their intent. Plus, there's a handy timeline at the back of the book to place the artists in context.

But that's not all; it's time for you to put down your preconceptions and pick up your pens to experiment with a whole range of different styles. Discover how easy (or difficult!) it is to create something in the style of your favourite modern artist in a few easy steps. You may even find your own artistic inspiration!

KOOKY Kandinsky

Wassily Kandinsky was the master of circles, squiggles and splodges. His technique may look easy at first glance, but that's part of his genius. He once said, "Of all the arts, abstract painting is the most difficult. It demands that you know how to draw well, that you have a heightened sensitivity for composition and for colour, and that you be a true poet."

Considered by some to be a trailblazer of Abstract Expressionism, the intensely spiritual Kandinsky saw his paintings as entire worlds, crafted to engage sight, sound and emotion. It's fair to say that boundaries were definitely not his thing.

Use these tips and template shapes as starting points to create your own Kandinsky-style art on the following pages.

shapes

Kandinsky used a variety of abstract shapes and lines to make his images.

GEOMETRIC SHAPES

CROSSHATCHING

FLUID LINES

DOTS

colours

method

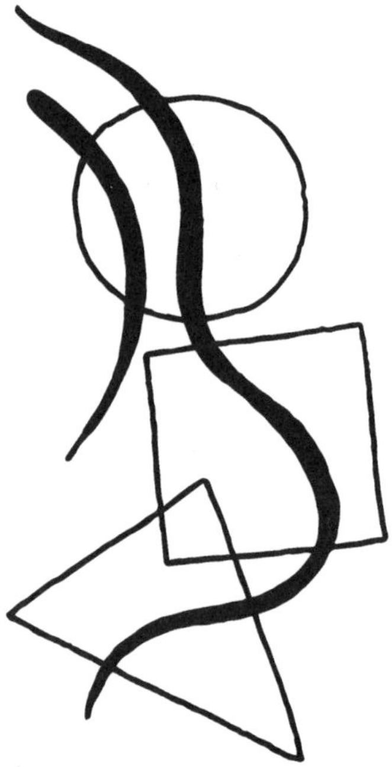

1. Dissect the shapes with a wiggly line or two.

2. Choose some Kandinsky-style shapes and details to add.

3. Colour some sections, and add final details in colour.

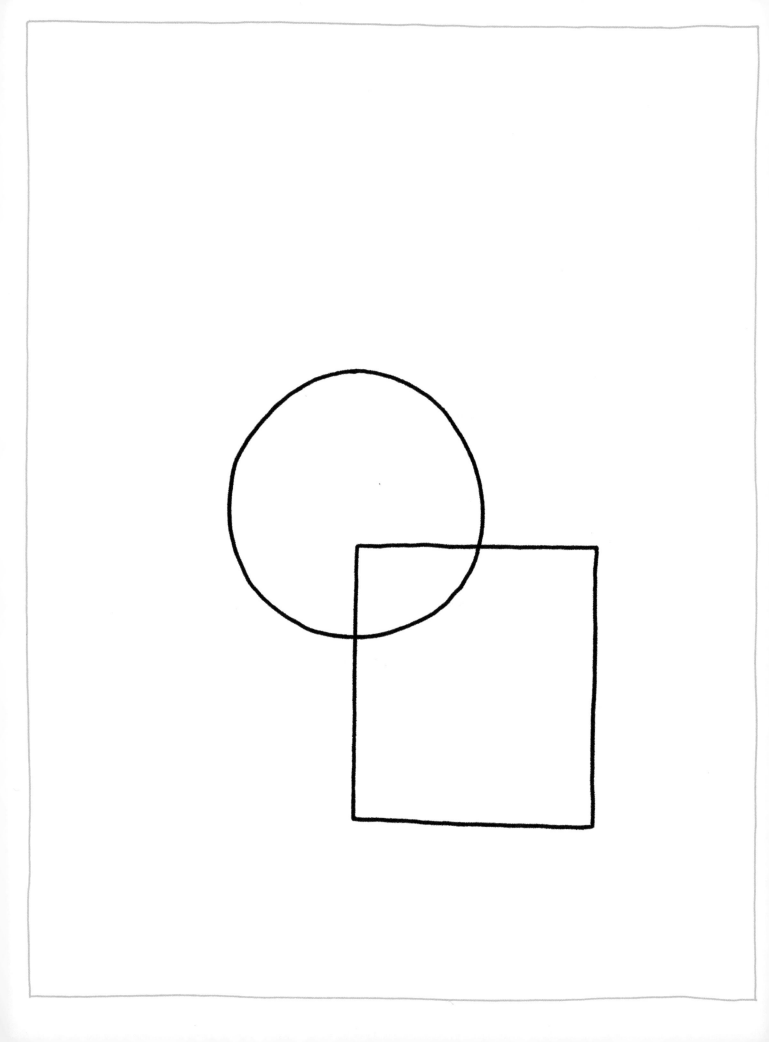

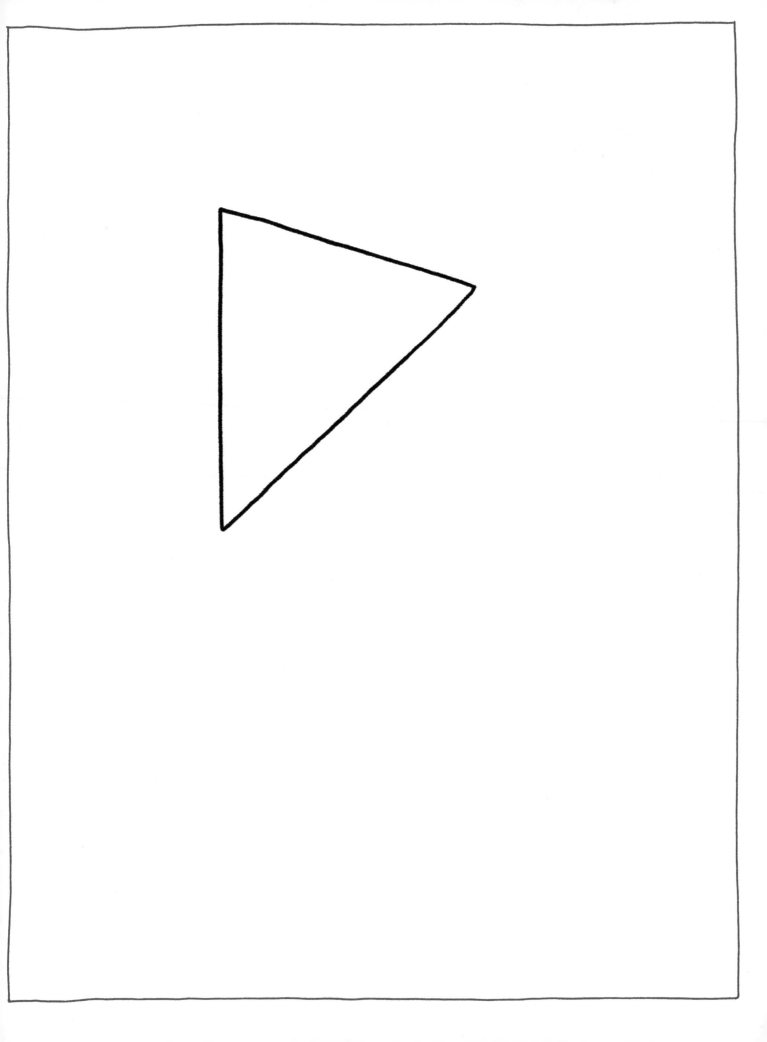

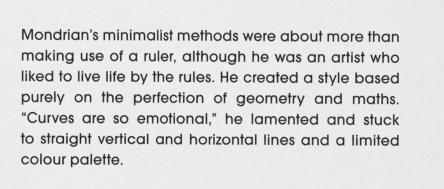

Mondrian

GRID

Mondrian's minimalist methods were about more than making use of a ruler, although he was an artist who liked to live life by the rules. He created a style based purely on the perfection of geometry and maths. "Curves are so emotional," he lamented and stuck to straight vertical and horizontal lines and a limited colour palette.

He is considered by many to be the founder of modern art, and helped to create a hugely successful art movement – De Stijl. However he left in disgust when another artist started using diagonal lines. Outrageous!

It may look simple, but a Mondrian-style grid is all about composition. He called it "a balance of unusual but equivalent oppositions."

the rules

While his 'stijl' changed throughout his career, Mondrian had some general rules for making his famous grid paintings that you can follow for yours:

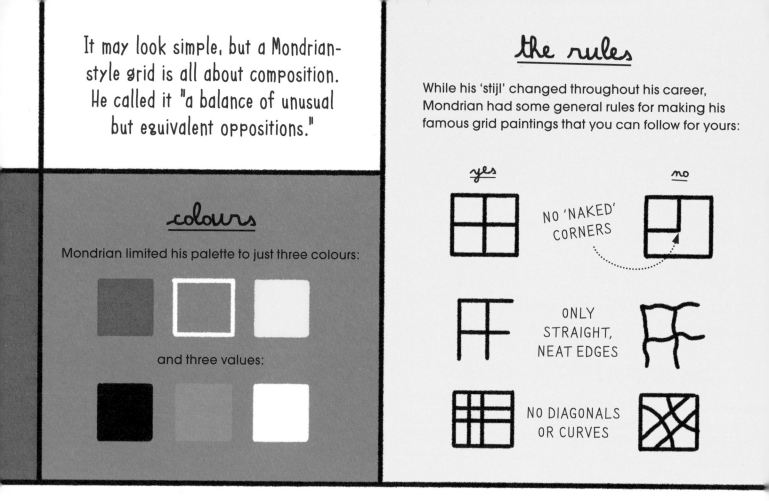

yes   no

NO 'NAKED' CORNERS

ONLY STRAIGHT, NEAT EDGES

NO DIAGONALS OR CURVES

colours

Mondrian limited his palette to just three colours:

and three values:

method

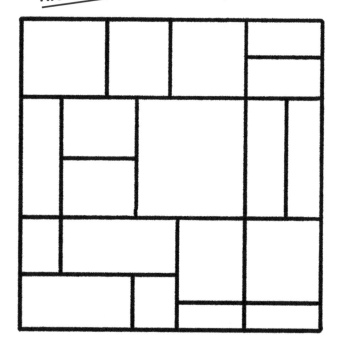

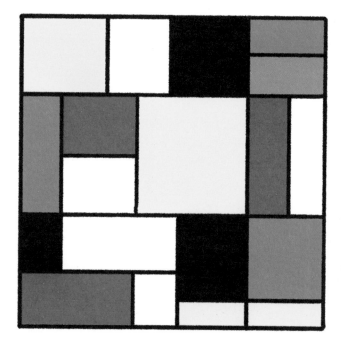

1. Using a ruler and thick black pen, divide the page using horizontal and vertical lines.

2. Colour in the boxes, remembering to use only Mondrian's favourite colours and values.

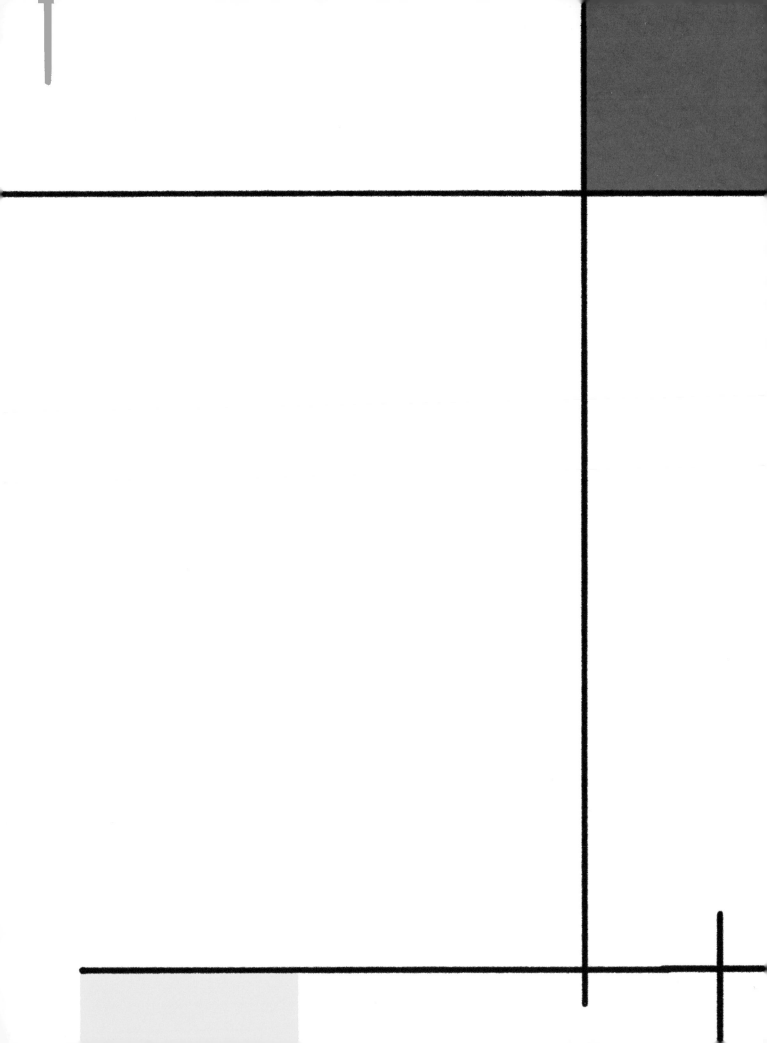

MIND—BENDING
RILEY

Whether you describe it as Op art, optical illusion or just plain old 'art that makes your eyes go funny', there's no doubting that Bridget Riley is one of the movement's leading lights. Her bold black and white graphics tapped into the psychedelic vibe of the swinging '60s and grabbed the attention of the public, even if it took the critics a while to catch on.

Riley experimented with geometric shapes to create disorientating patterns that seem to change colour or even move. If there was a place where art and magic collide, that place would surely be the spiritual home of Riley's hypnotizing work.

Follow the steps and discover how the simplest idea can have electrifying results.

THE RED LINE INDICATES YOUR STARTING POINT

method

1. Start with four circles.

2. In black, draw a zigzag line from the outermost to the innermost circle.

3. Repeat the zigzag around the circle, keeping the distance between lines roughly the same but altering the angle each time. The lines should get closer together towards the centre of the circle.

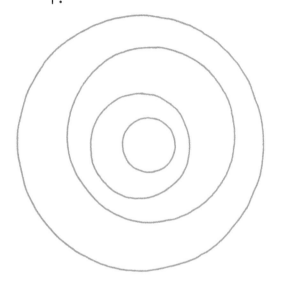

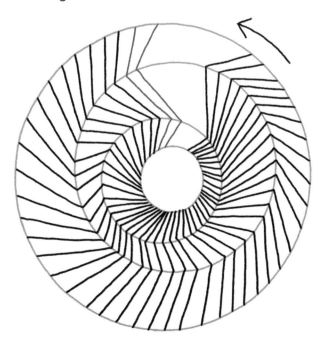

4. Colour in alternating black and white sections between the rows and circles.

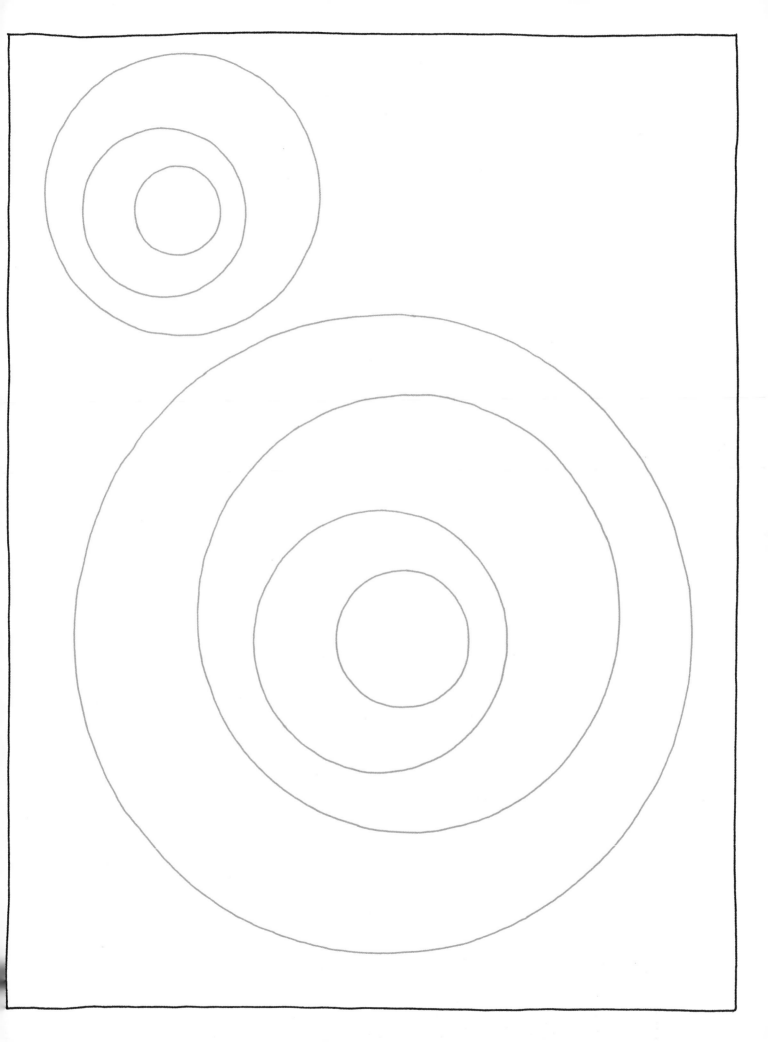

WEIRD & WONDERFUL
Magritte

Apples, clouds and men in bowler hats might seem like pretty standard subjects for your average artist – but René Magritte was anything but average. The Belgian Surrealist's aim was to "make the most everyday objects shriek aloud." And, in some of his work, those ordinary objects were positively yelling from the rooftops.

Magritte's approach was to take surreal ideas and paint them in a highly realistic style. The end result is a series of haunting, otherworldly pieces that spark the imagination and stick in the mind.

Use random objects in place of facial features for a portrait that will make everyone take a second glance.

method

1. Pick a face shape.

2. Add round objects for eyes.

3. Add a long object for the nose.

4. Add a wide object for the mouth.

5. Top it off with a bowler hat.

6. Colour!

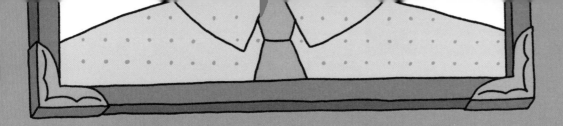

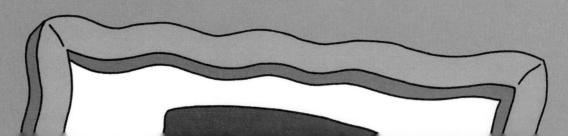

HARING

GRAFFITI
DOODLE

Walls, ceilings and subway trains were the preferred canvases of Keith Haring. Influenced by Pop art, graffiti and street culture, his vibrant, pared-back pictures took the New York art scene by storm, and spread important messages about racism, drug abuse and AIDS.

Haring's signature images, created with bright colours and bold outlines, included dancing figures, TVs, dogs, hearts and crawling babies. Haring once said, "Children know something that most people have forgotten." So, it's time to cast your mind back to the trademark pictures you drew again and again at school, and recreate them in colourful and energetic combinations.

colours

Haring used brightly-coloured paint, but you can use pencils or felt tips.

symbols

method

MOVEMENT LINES

1. Draw around the outside of the stick people with black marker, adding blobs for hands.

2. Add movement lines.

3. Fill the space between the figures with a mixture of fun symbols.

4. Add colour.

Arp

SIMPLE SPLODGES

Hans Arp was nothing if not versatile. Not happy with just one medium, he excelled at sculpting, painting, drawing and poetry. He wasn't even content with just one name, calling himself Hans when speaking in German and Jean when speaking in French.

Perhaps the most remarkable of Arp's works are his 'chance pictures'. "Everything must be pulled apart," he once said, which is literally how he created these pieces, dropping torn-out shapes onto paper and pasting them where they fell. The loose, wobbly forms conjure images of nature, but are highly open to interpretation. When looking at Arp's unique creations, what do you see?

Arp's art was based around the rejection of traditional ideas of beauty. So don't be afraid to draw something weird ...

colours

shapes

Arp was a biomorphist, which meant he used lots of rounded shapes.

WIGGLY

BLOBBY

method

1. Trace over the shape with black marker, then add a second wiggly shape below.

2. Choose a colour and draw a large, blobby shape that flows behind the wiggly outlines.

3. Fill in the black outlines in solid black and the coloured outlines in their matching colour. Fill the rest of the page with a third colour.

DELAUNAY
GEOMETRICS

Sonia Delaunay's jazzed-up geometrics brought life to everything from canvases and costumes to theatre and fashion. Alongside her husband and fellow artistic ground-breaker, Robert Delaunay, she was a founder of Orphism – a striking method of mixing bold curves of primary and secondary colours.

Looking at Delaunay's work is often like gazing into a kaleidoscope, and it seems that is how she herself saw the world. "Colour is the skin of the world," she once said, and after admiring her myriad of masterpieces it's hard to disagree.

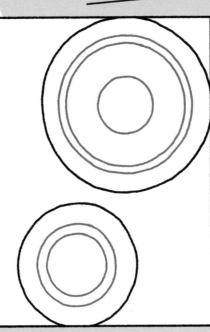

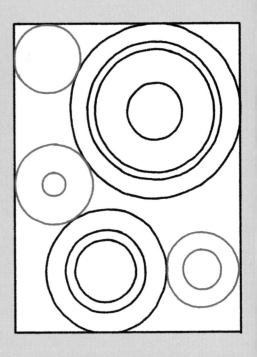

Delaunay's interest in colour theory helped inform her designs. With a few pointers you can experiment, too.

colours

1. Use a pair of compasses or draw around some round objects to add two or three small circles inside the larger ones.

2. Fill the gaps on the page with more circles. Make them as large as possible, so they touch each other.

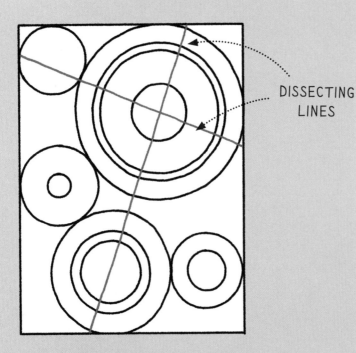

DISSECTING LINES

3. In pencil, draw a diagonal line running top to bottom, and one running right to left. The lines should dissect at least one circle.

4. Colour each section in a bright colour. Don't use the same colour for adjacent sections.

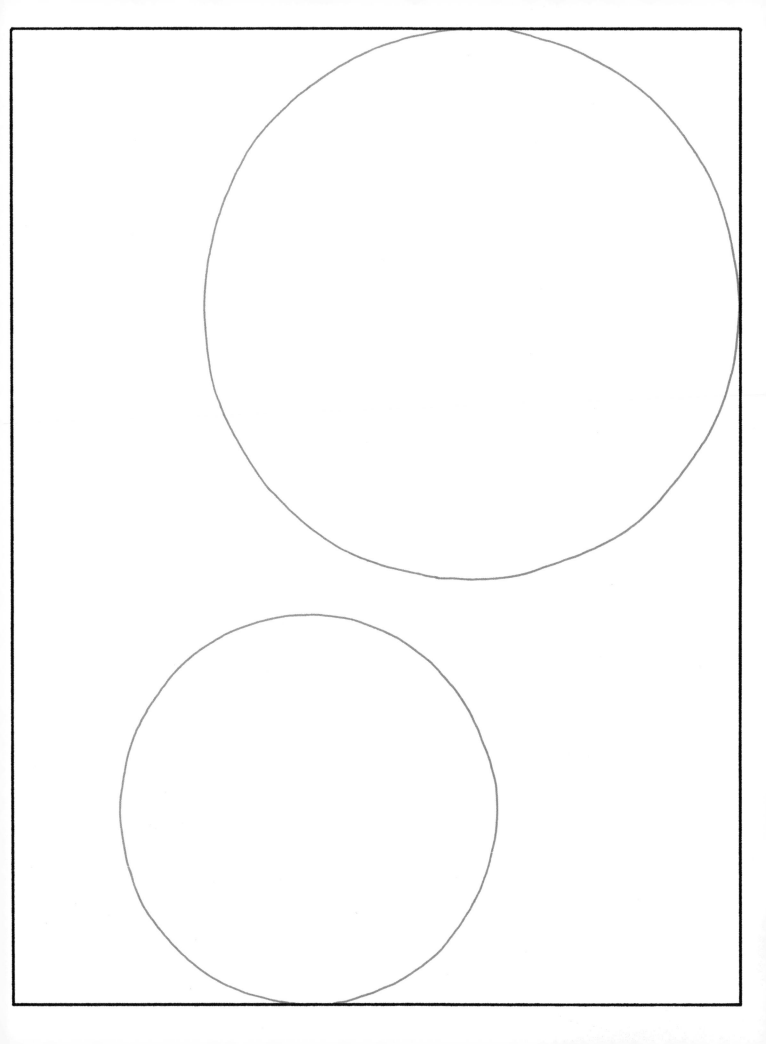

BIOMORPHIC Miró

Joan Miró's art career got off to a bad start in his Spanish homeland when his first ever exhibition was ridiculed by critics and the public alike ... but what do they know, right? Miró had the last laugh when he upped sticks, moved to Paris and became one of the pioneers of Surrealism.

His vivid, abstract works, characterized by energetic lines and bold colours may look simple, but as Miró himself once said, "Yes, it took me just a moment to draw this line with the brush. But it took me months, perhaps even years, of reflection to form the idea."

BLOBS & DETAILS

shapes

Miró used long, thin lines that flowed all over the page. He added blobs and shapes in colour, as well as smaller decorative details.

SWIRLY LINES

colours

method

1. Add more swirly lines with decorative flourishes, such as spirals and zigzags.

2. Choose some blobs and shapes to add on top of the lines.

3. Fill the shapes with colour. Add extra details to fill the gaps.

Fang Zhaoling

FOREST

Merging traditional Chinese art styles with a contemporary social conscience, Fang Zhaoling was behind some of the most engrossing landscape art of her generation. As a teenager she studied calligraphy, and it shows in the dramatic strokes she used to create trees, rocks and mountains.

Fang was something of a late bloomer, taking up painting in her late thirties and continually developing her style over the 50 years that followed. A common trope of her output was huge, hulking scenes sheltering tiny, caricature-like figures, giving her work an imposing, almost overwhelming feel. This is abstract art at its most thoughtful.

Fang Zhaoling combined traditional calligraphy with more modern influences. Now you can, too!

 method

 SPIKY BRANCHES

1. Thicken the tree branches with black marker, making them wider at the base than the tip.

2. Add some thinner, spiky branches, leaving room in between to draw the blossom.

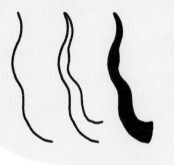

FLOWERS

3. Add flower shapes to the branches in pink or red.

4. Add some caricature-like figures below the trees, if you fancy.

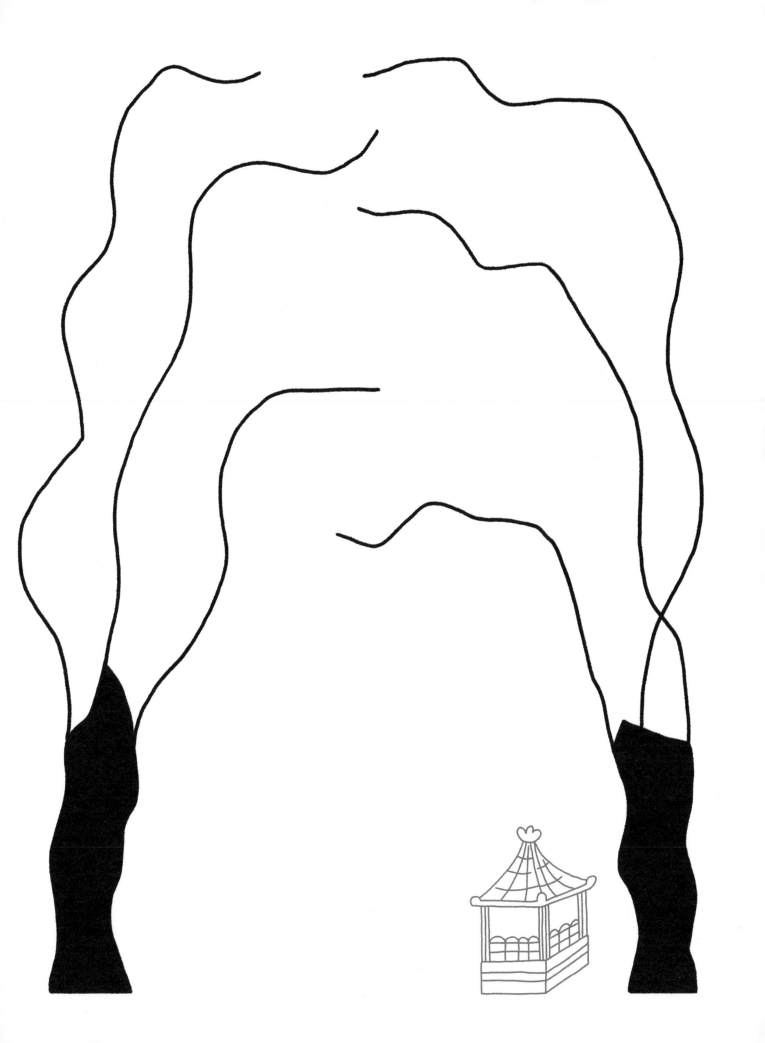

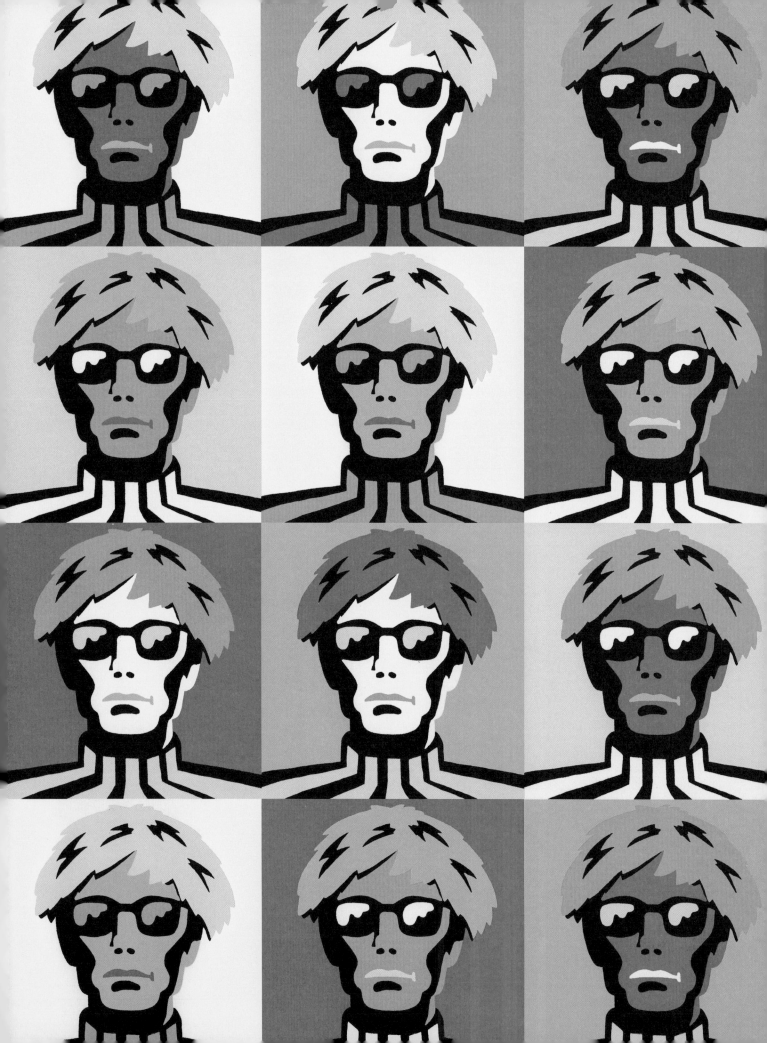

POP Like WARHOL

Andy Warhol famously said, "art is what you can get away with" – and he got away with a lot! This bewigged founding father of the Pop art movement used everything from bananas to cans of Campbell's soup to create vibrant and relatable prints that brought art to the people.

But perhaps the thing he's best known for (aside from his raucous parties and A-lister friends) is his striking silkscreen portrait of Marilyn Monroe. Like Monroe, Warhol is no longer with us, but his incredible impact on pop culture lives on.

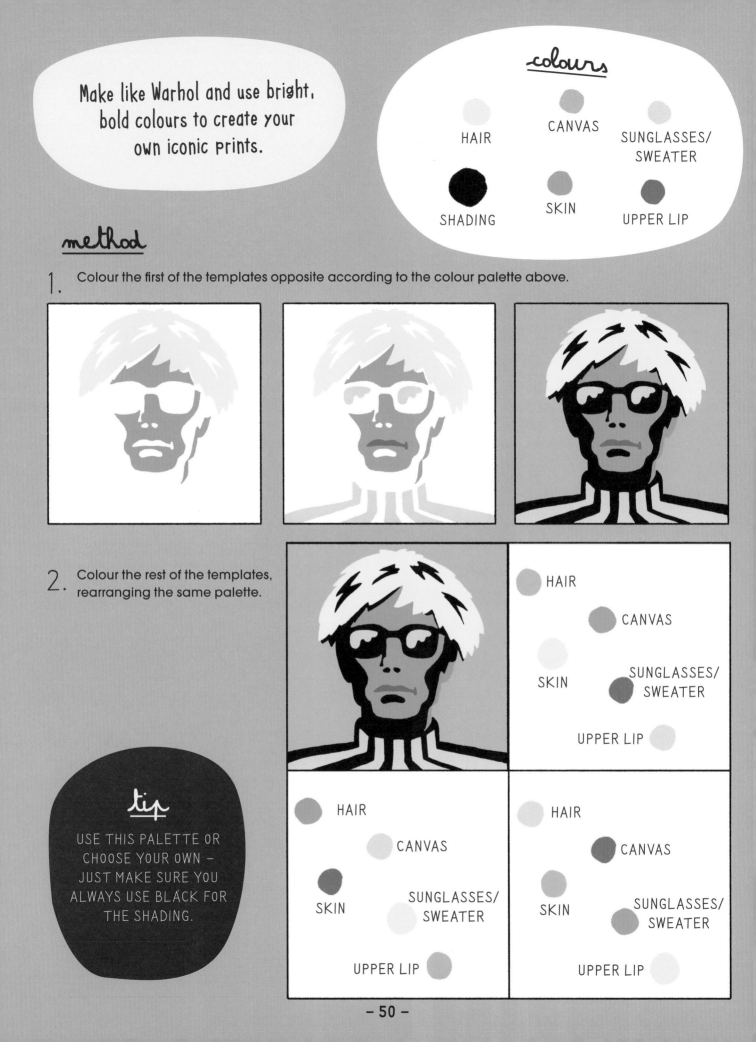

Make like Warhol and use bright, bold colours to create your own iconic prints.

colours

HAIR

CANVAS

SUNGLASSES/ SWEATER

SHADING

SKIN

UPPER LIP

method

1. Colour the first of the templates opposite according to the colour palette above.

2. Colour the rest of the templates, rearranging the same palette.

HAIR

CANVAS

SKIN

SUNGLASSES/ SWEATER

UPPER LIP

HAIR

CANVAS

SKIN

SUNGLASSES/ SWEATER

UPPER LIP

HAIR

CANVAS

SKIN

SUNGLASSES/ SWEATER

UPPER LIP

tip

USE THIS PALETTE OR CHOOSE YOUR OWN – JUST MAKE SURE YOU ALWAYS USE BLACK FOR THE SHADING.

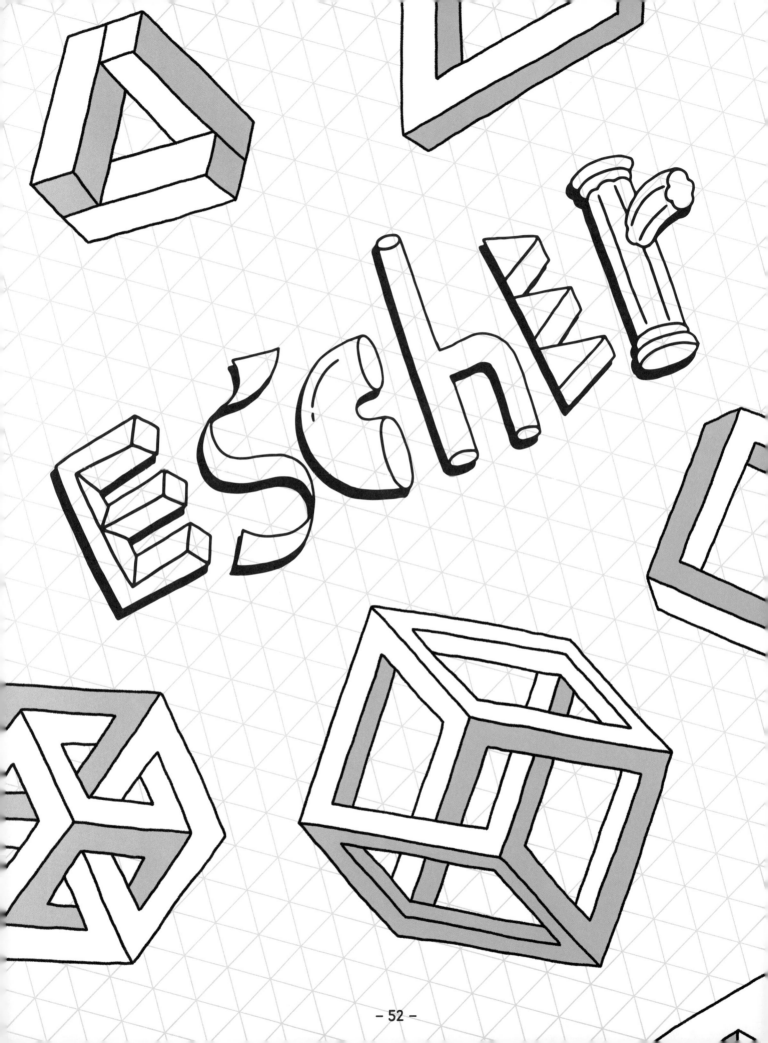

IMPOSSIBLE CONSTRUCTION

Is it a floor? Is it a ceiling? With the work of Dutch graphic artist M.C. Escher, you can never quite tell. His mind-boggling, reality-warping constructions turn perspectives upside-down and inside-out to create a world that is as beautiful as it is unsettling. If it feels like your eyes are deceiving you, it might well be because they are.

Much of Escher's work features impossibly interlocking staircases, which directly inspired the visuals in a number of hit movies, ranging from *Labyrinth* to *Interstellar*. His art is sometimes deceptively simple, sometimes engrossingly complex, but always challenging.

Use the triangular grid to guide the positioning of your lines and help you recreate this mind-boggling masterpiece.

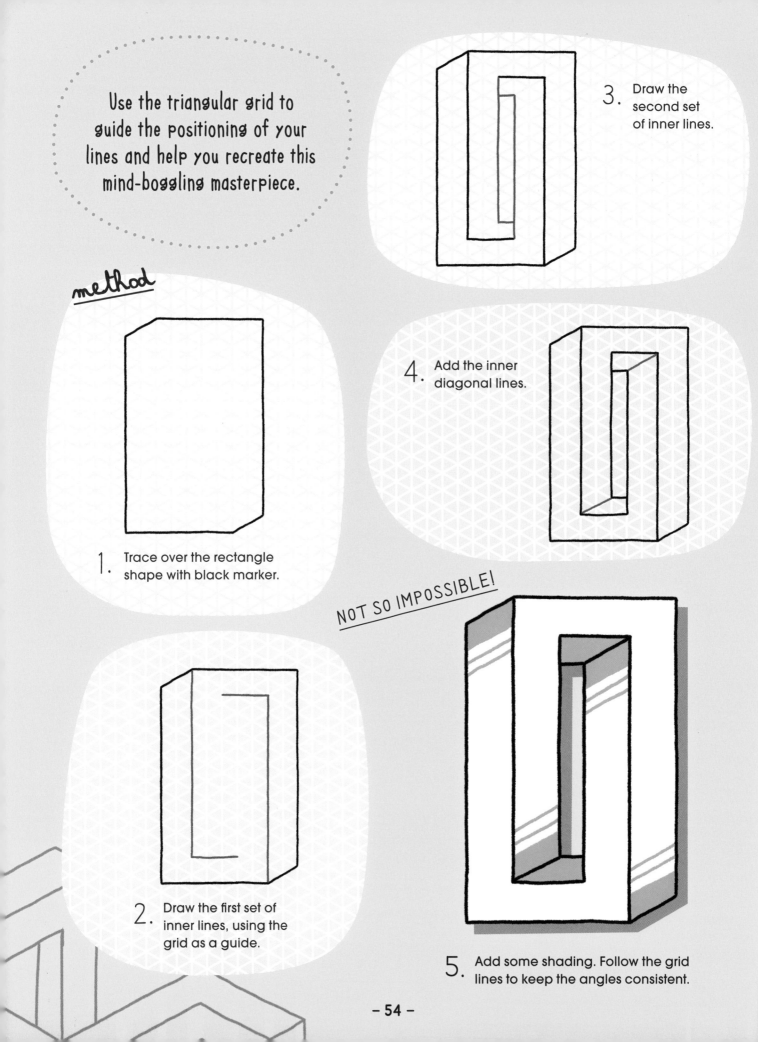

method

1. Trace over the rectangle shape with black marker.

2. Draw the first set of inner lines, using the grid as a guide.

3. Draw the second set of inner lines.

4. Add the inner diagonal lines.

NOT SO IMPOSSIBLE!

5. Add some shading. Follow the grid lines to keep the angles consistent.

Radical Af Klint

Arguably Europe's first abstract artist, Hilma af Klint was all about opposites. In much of her work, the geometric collides with the organic. She often preferred delicate colours, but on vast canvases. She was a student of maths and science, but was also a conductor of spooky seances. She also shunned exhibitions and the public eye, yet at the same time kept detailed notebooks to explain the symbols she created.

At her own request, her masterpieces remained locked away unseen for 20 years after her death – which poses the question of how much more great art from a bygone era could be out there, waiting to be discovered.

Af klint rarely exhibited her work, but you'll want
to share your abstract imagery far and wide.

colours

method

USE TWO COLOURS
FOR EACH CIRCLE

shapes

1. In pencil, fill the circles
with af Klint-style shapes.

2. Colour the shapes in
constrasting shades. Add
a pale background colour.

ANCHOR YOUR
LOOPING LINES
TO THE EDGE OF
THE PAGE.

patterns

3. With black marker, add
looping lines around the
outside of the page.

4. Fill inside the shapes with patterns.

BRIGHT AND BOLD

Léger

Roll up, roll up! Fernand Léger absolutely loved the circus, and it shows in his work. "Go to the circus," he once said, "It is so human to break through restraints, to spread out, to grow toward freedom … To escape from the ground, to leave it, to touch the tip as little as possible, the farthest tip."

This French Cubist loved primary colours, bold lines and funky patterns. His sprawling portfolio encompassed films, ceramics, book illustration and even theatre sets. Fighting in World War I shifted his focus from the human to the industrial, but the liveliness of his work remained a constant.

Recreate Léger's personal form of Cubism
with this bright, blocky portrait.

method

1. Add extra strips of colour to the page.

2. Use a black marker to draw a head and neck.

3. Add some eyes. Don't draw them too close to the top.

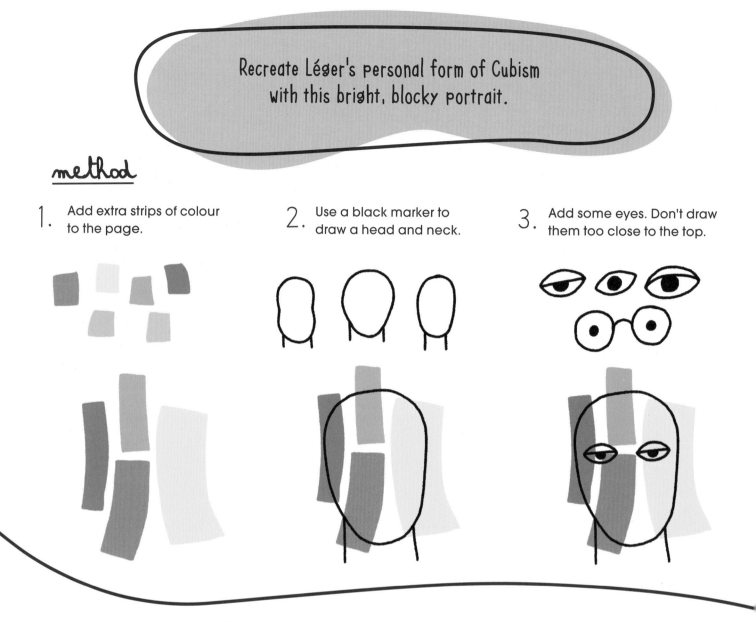

4. Draw the nose and eyebrows as one continuous line.

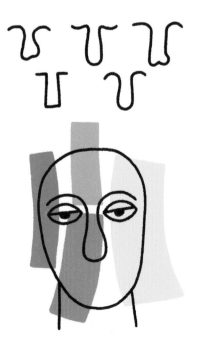

5. Add some lips. Join them to the nose with a line.

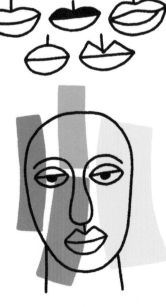

6. Finish by choosing a hairstyle and adding ears.

GRAPHIC
GONCharova

Never one to shy away from controversy, Natalia Goncharova was willing to do whatever it took to get her work out there. At her most extreme, she would cover her body in paint and parade through the streets – quite literally making an exhibition of herself. She even stood trial for pornography for her paintings of nudes, but was acquitted.

Don't let the media circus fool you. Goncharova was highly skilled, mastering multiple styles and co-creating a movement of her own, called Rayonism. Taking influence from the folk art of her Russian homeland, she created raw, vibrant pieces that explode with colour.

Goncharova used bright, contrasting colours and angular shapes, inspired by the folk art of her native Russia.

method

1. Draw stems coming out of the vase.

2. Add green shapes to the ends of the stems.

3. Add different green shapes along the stems.

4. Fill the gaps around the outside of the page with red shapes.

5. Fill the background with a complementary colour.

Murakami

FLOWER POWER

Growing up in the Japan of the 1960s and '70s, Takashi Murakami was exposed to a whirlwind of influences. On one hand, the aftermath of the atomic bomb that was dropped on Nagasaki in 1945, on the other, the artistic styles of anime, manga and kawaii. So it's probably no surprise that his work feels like a smashing together of Pop art and subculture.

In Murakami's Superflat movement, cutesie flowers in bubblegum colours inhabit the same world as over-sized body parts, jaws lined with razor-sharp teeth and ominous skulls. Love it or hate it, it's a unique style that is instantly recognisable as pure Murakami.

Crack a smile as you recreate Murakami's shiny, happy flower scene.

colours

method

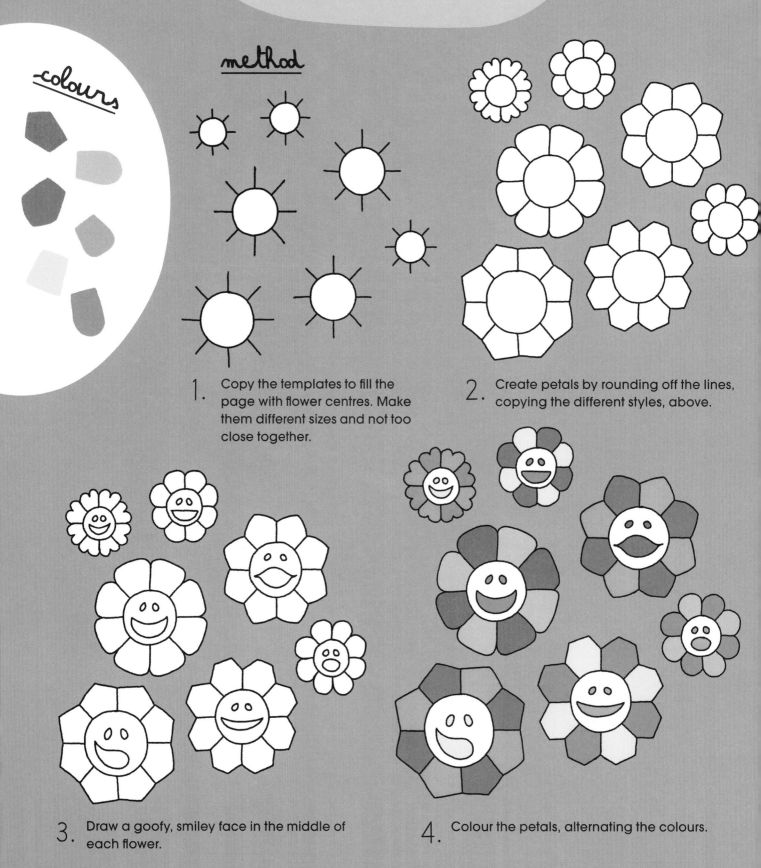

1. Copy the templates to fill the page with flower centres. Make them different sizes and not too close together.

2. Create petals by rounding off the lines, copying the different styles, above.

3. Draw a goofy, smiley face in the middle of each flower.

4. Colour the petals, alternating the colours.

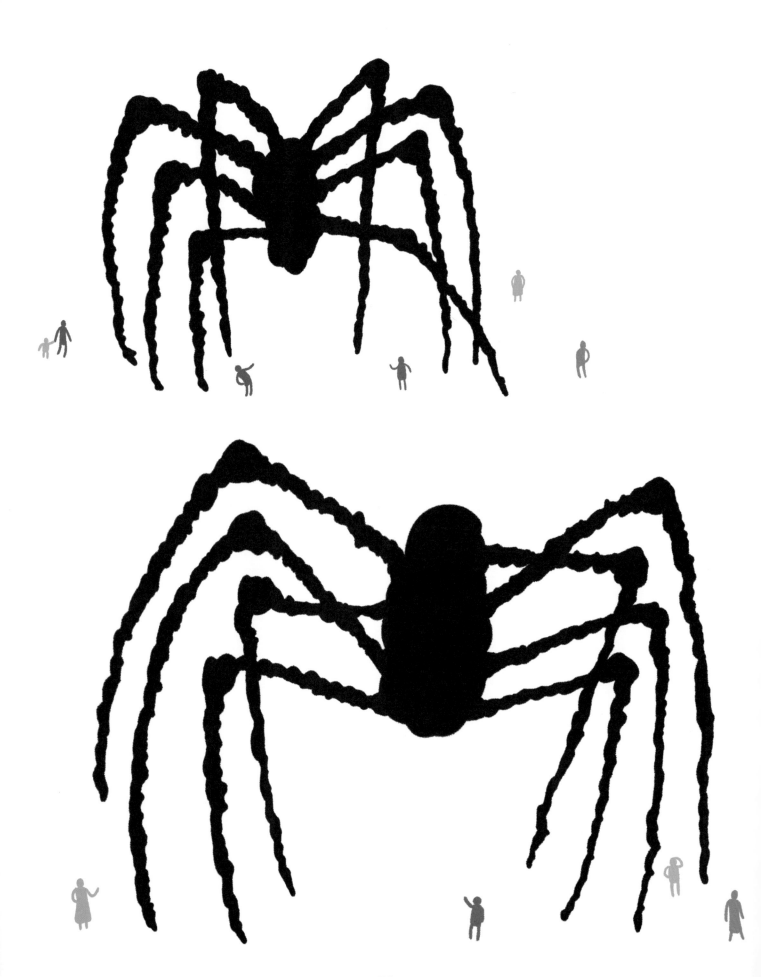

BOURGEOIS
SUPERSIZE SPIDERS

Arachnophobes look away now! Louise Bourgeois was a super-sculptor who created spiders so big that they'd often fill an entire room. Terrifying.

Although she didn't produce the first of her famous spider sculptures until she was in her eighties, her spidery senses tingled from early on in her career. Amazing arachnids were a focus of many of her early prints and drawings, and she even compared the eight-legged beasties to her own mother. "Why the spider? Because my best friend was my mother and she was deliberate, clever, patient, soothing, reasonable, dainty, subtle, indispensable, neat, and as useful as a spider."

This sketchy two-dimensional spider is surely less scary than Bourgeois's giant sculptures.

method

1. Scribble a rounded rectangle shape in the middle of the page with black marker.

BODY

3. Draw more squiggly lines to create lower legs, descending from the upper legs.

2. Draw some upper legs using squiggly, looping strokes. Add a more solid blob at each end.

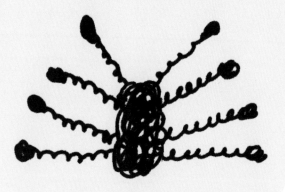

4. Fill in the gaps in your squiggles. Don't make it too neat.

FILL IN THESE BITS ...

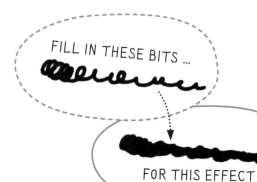

FOR THIS EFFECT

BASQUIAT

SCRIBBLE SKULL

Scribbles, scrawls and scratches … rebel artist Jean-Michel Basquiat would never win awards for colouring inside the lines, but he can take credit for transforming street art into high art in 1980s America.

Don't worry if you skipped art lessons, Basquiat himself admitted, "I failed the art courses I did take in school." Yet without formal training he sold works for millions of dollars and got to hang out with Andy Warhol and his famous friends. Using paint, collage and graffiti, Basquiat created many self-portraits, often adding a crown to his head to show everyone that he was the king of the underground art scene.

Inspired? Over to you …

Basquiat didn't try to stay
inside the lines when drawing
his scribbly skulls.

colours

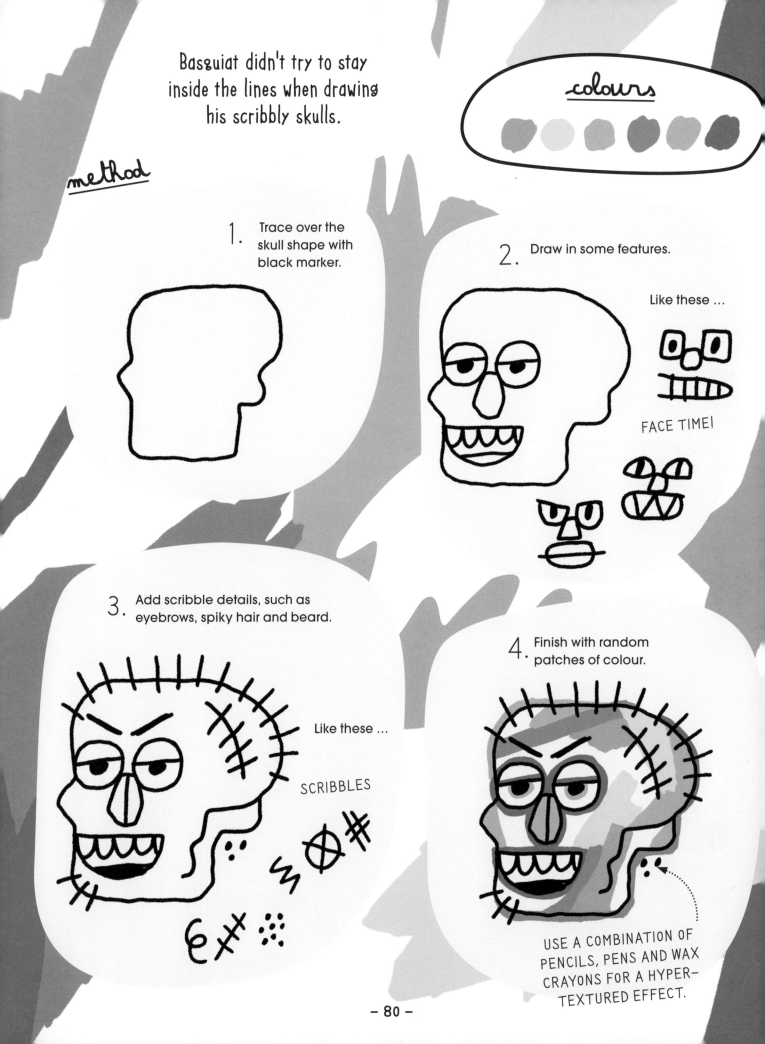

method

1. Trace over the
skull shape with
black marker.

2. Draw in some features.

Like these ...

FACE TIME!

3. Add scribble details, such as
eyebrows, spiky hair and beard.

Like these ...

SCRIBBLES

4. Finish with random
patches of colour.

USE A COMBINATION OF
PENCILS, PENS AND WAX
CRAYONS FOR A HYPER-
TEXTURED EFFECT.

– 80 –

Picasso FACES

Cubism brings different views of subjects together in the same picture to suggest their three-dimensional form. They appear fragmented and abstract. The most famous of the Cubists was Pablo Picasso.

"A head," said Picasso, "is a matter of eyes, nose, mouth, which can be distributed in any way you like." His portraits often feature a combination of forwards and sideways-facing features. The beauty of Cubism is that it's not supposed to be realistic, so you can let your imagination run wild.

Cubism means drawing something from more than one point of view, so get ready to break the rules.

method

1. Trace over the head shape with black marker.

2. Draw a line down the middle, with a nose facing right.

3. On the left side, add sideways features ...

4. On the right side, draw the front features ...

... like these

FRONT FEATURES

5. Add colour.

... like these

SIDE FEATURES

tip

DRAW THE SECOND MOUTH OVER THE MIDDLE LINE, FOR EXTRA WEIRDNESS.

TAKE FLIGHT LIKE
BRAQUE

Alongside his BFF Pablo Picasso, Georges Braque was the co-creator of Cubism, an abstract art movement that shows different perspectives at the same time. Braque also dipped his toes in the waters of Impressionism, Expressionism and Fauvism, and he even invented his own collage style called *papier collé*. However, it's his numerous bird pieces that really spring to mind upon mention of his name.

Braque's birds have been said to represent peace, hope and even the nature of art itself. He once said, "art is made to disturb," but, as his own work proves, it can also delight.

method

Soar to new artistic heights with this pair of bold and beautiful birds.

STARS & MOONS

1. Trace over the body templates with a black marker pen.

KEEP YOUR DRAWINGS NAÏVE AND FREE.

2. Draw two loose crescent shapes with one zigzag edge halfway along the body shapes.

3. Fill in the shapes with black, then switch to a coloured pen to draw an outline around the birds.

4. Add some star and moon shapes.

5. Fill in the rest of the page with the same colour you used to outline the birds.

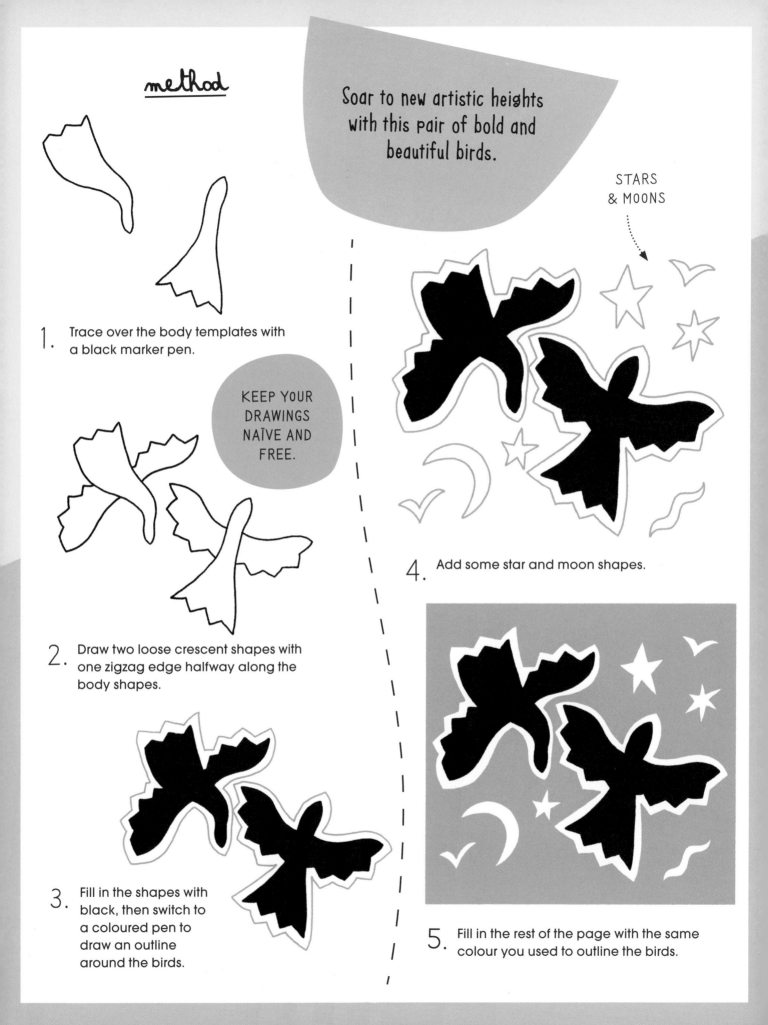

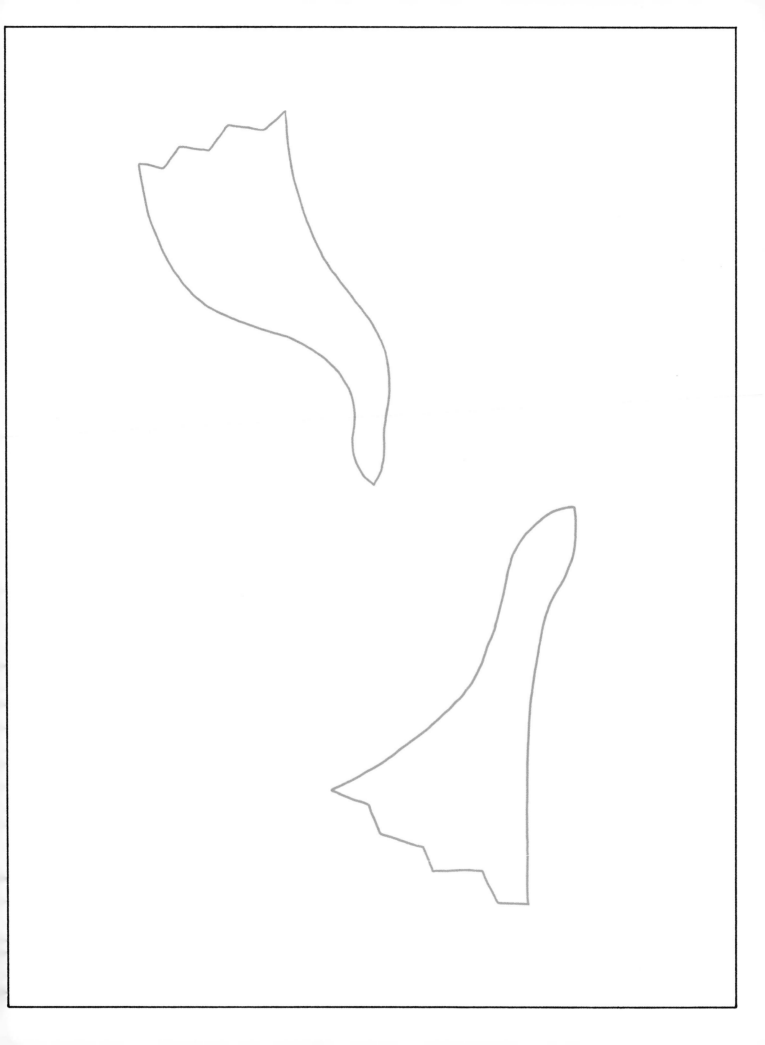

MYTHICAL Mora

Mirka Mora's fun, childlike murals belie her own traumatic back story. As a teenager, she escaped from a Nazi imprisonment camp and spent several years hiding in the forests of France. She had little education or artistic training, but upon emigrating to Melbourne as an adult, she truly blossomed.

She excelled at painting and sculpting, often peppering her work with cherubic characters and mythical creatures. Despite her distressing background, she treasured childhood and clung to it through her art. She once said, "If you grow up and be an adult you have to leave it behind. That would be terrible. I couldn't do that."

Copy Mora's wide-eyed faces to make your own dreamy mural.

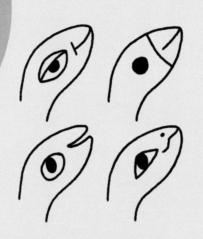

1. Add face and wing details to the bird.

2. Choose facial expressions to add to the circles.

3. Fill the gaps with quirky details. Colour in.

Swirling Van Gogh sky

Vincent van Gogh could be the ultimate role model for anyone who feels they have a tortured, misunderstood genius somewhere inside them just waiting to burst out. He famously sold just one painting during his life, but has since become one of art's most iconic names.

"If you hear a voice within you say 'you cannot paint', then by all means paint, and that voice will be silenced," he once said. He followed his own advice and created swirling masterpieces of wheat fields, sunflowers, starry nights and dozens of self-portraits. The lesson? Don't be embarrassed if people don't appreciate your artwork. They'll catch up eventually.

Van Gogh loved the contrast between blue and yellow, and often combined the two colours in his paintings.

method

1. In pencil, draw two long, swirling lines, flowing around the moon and stars.

SWIRLING LINES

MOON & STARS

2. Fill in the three sections with three shades of blue. Colour the stars and the moon in bright yellow.

SKY COLOURS

WIGGLY DASHES

3. Using a darker blue, make short, dashed marks on top of the blue sky, following the shape of the swirling lines.

Dubuffet

HEAD

What drives an artist? For Jean Dubuffet, the answer was simple: "instinct, passion, mood, violence, madness." This complex character shunned academic art in favour of outsider art, or 'art brut' as he called it. So, where others have been inspired by the greats, Dubuffet took his lead from children, prisoners and the mentally ill.

Dubuffet's aim was to appeal to the 'everyman', and his iconic style originated from that most ordinary of media, the ballpoint pen. Using simple red, blue and black ink, what started out as absent-minded doodling swiftly grew into a multi-million pound body of work.

Recreate Dubuffet's famous loose, fluid style by following these simple steps.

features

method

1. Add shoulders and ears to the potato-shaped head.

2. Draw in facial features and add shirt details to the shoulders.

tip
KEEP THESE ELEMENTS AS SIMPLE AS POSSIBLE.

3. Section off random areas within the face and body to create an abstract, patchwork effect.

4. Choose a pattern or colour to fill each section. Leave some empty if you like.

patterns

colours

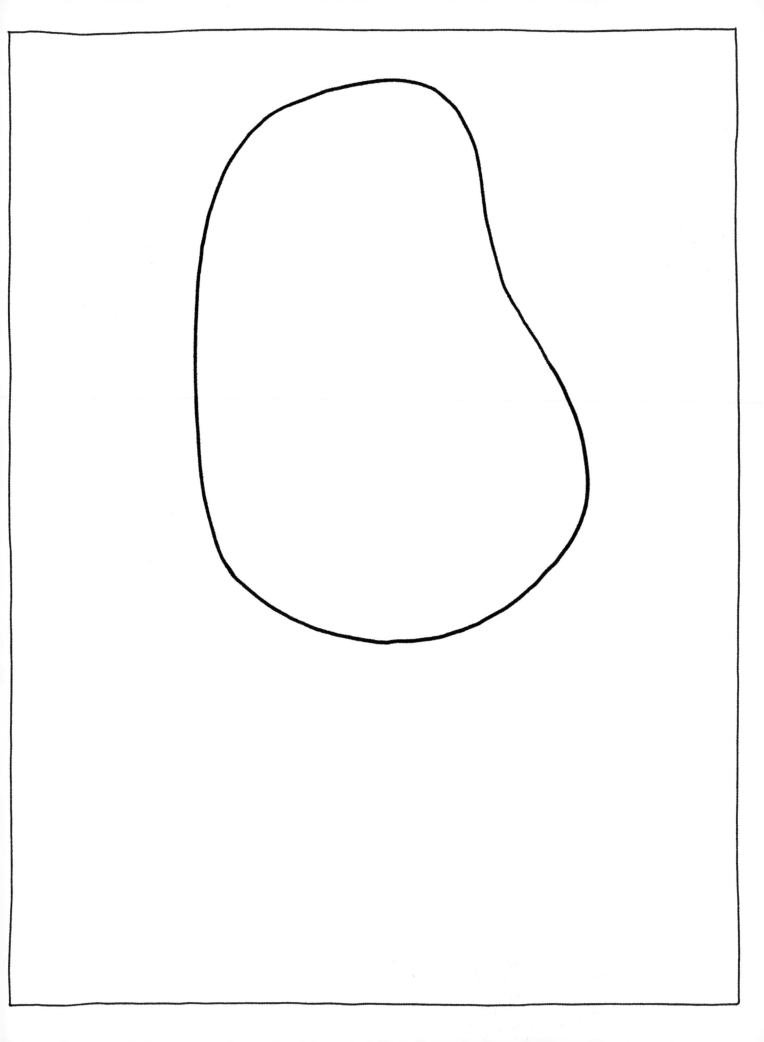

STÖLZL

PATTERNS

Gunta Stölzl's wondrous weaving changed the face of textile design forever. A key figure in the emergence of Germany's famous Bauhaus art school, she went from student to teacher, heading up the weaving department and revolutionizing textile techniques in the process. She was also Bauhaus's first female 'master', but it is for her own art rather than her teaching that she is truly remembered.

Stölzl experimented with geometric forms that at times seem illogical and break their own rules. The resulting tapestries are an almost hypnotic explosion of colours, shapes and patterns that many have tried to copy, but few could ever match.

Stölzl worked with textiles and weaving, so much of her work follows lines and gridded sections, with complementary patterns.

method

colours

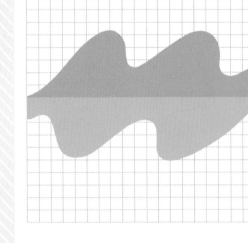

1. Colour the two shapes, the top half in one colour and the bottom half in a contrasting colour.

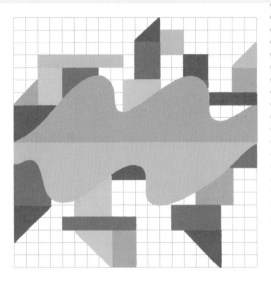

2. Use the grid as a guide to fill the page with squares, rectangles and triangles. Colour them as you go.

3. Keep going until the page is full. Try not to fill adjacent shapes with the same colour.

4. Use a black pen to fill some of the shapes with patterns.

patterns

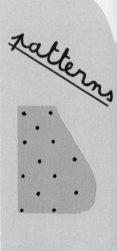

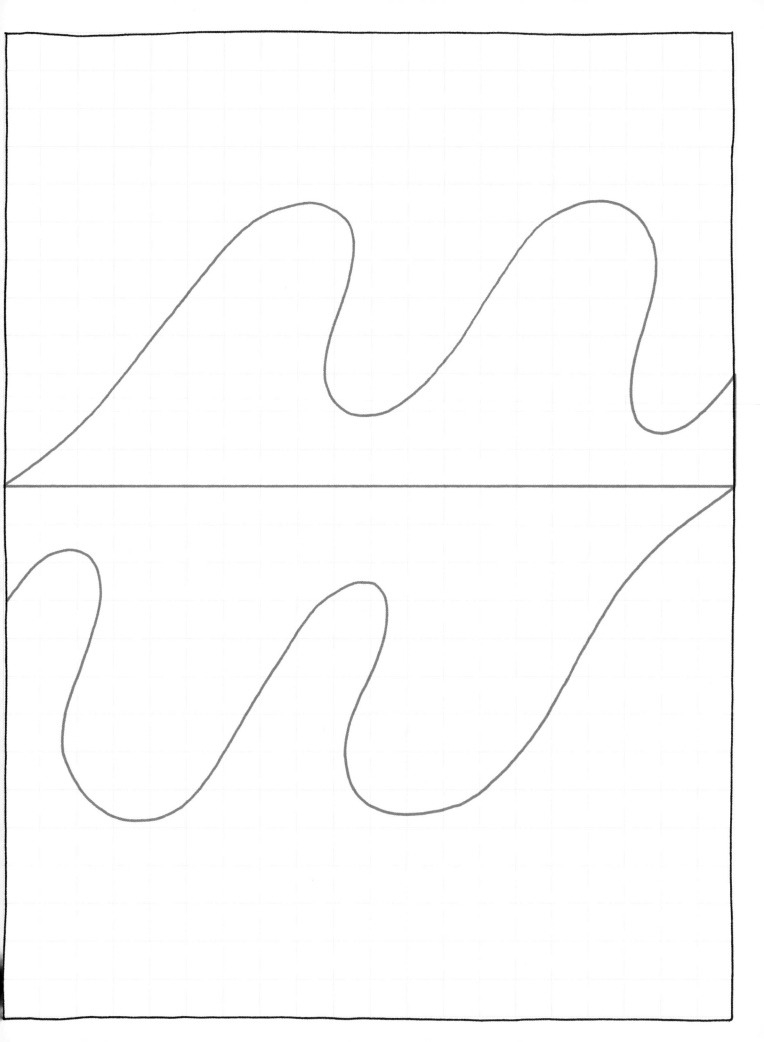

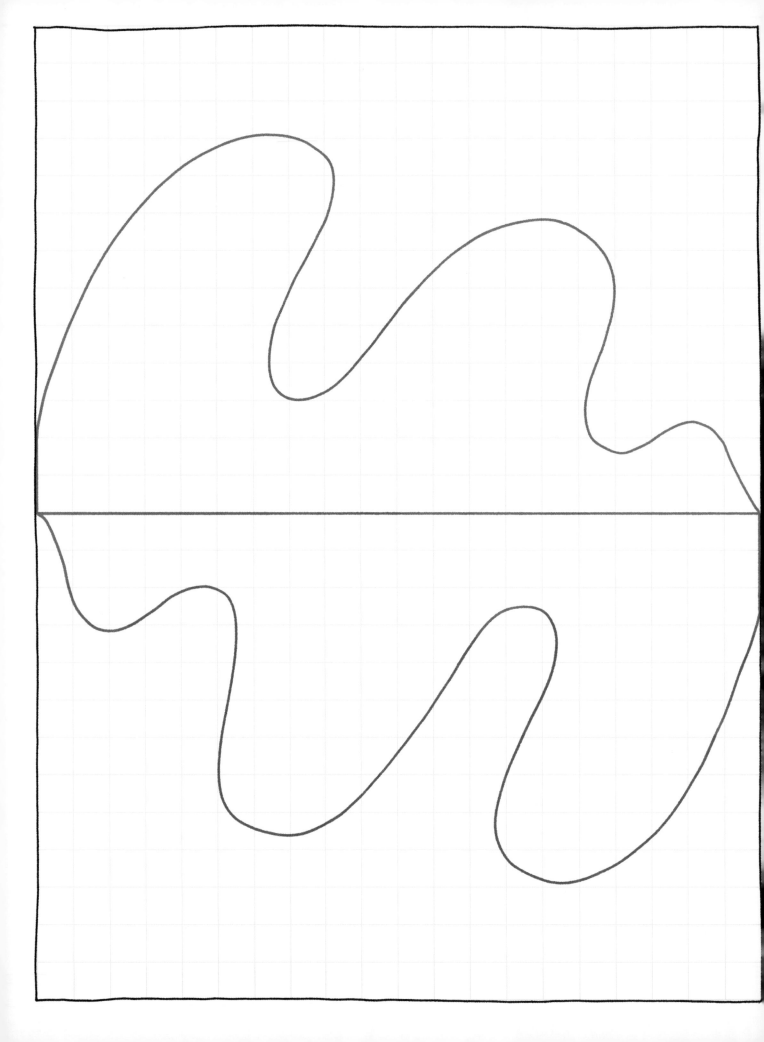

Krasner

SYMBOLS

Looking like hieroglyphics gone wild, Lee Krasner's Abstract Expressionism seems to invite us to decipher a language that will never be revealed. She believed art should be bold and energetic, preferably with paint squeezed straight from the tube. "I like a canvas to breathe and be alive," she once said. "Be alive is the point."

When she took a disliking to her own work, she'd cut it up and use the pieces to make new collages, both destroying and creating at the same time. In fact, she did this with so much of her art that, sadly, much of it is lost forever.

Krasner was an admirer of Mondrian and was inspired by his 'grid' to create her own abstract artwork, based around straight lines.

shapes

Krasner used 'scrambles' of dark, muted colours and geometric lines to fill her canvas.

colours

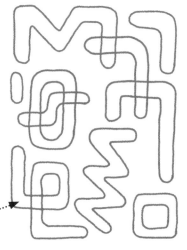

method

1. Use a pencil to fill the page with overlapping 'worm' shapes.

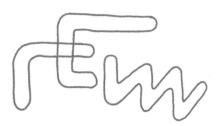

2. Use lots of different shapes, leaving only small gaps between them.

tip

USE THE GRID TO HELP KEEP THE LINES STRAIGHT AND THEIR WIDTHS CONSISTENT.

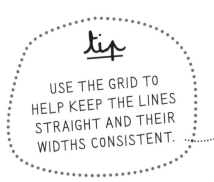

3. Colour random sections of the surrounding grid, leaving the shapes white.

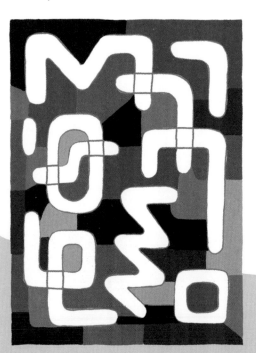

4. Rub out your pencil lines.

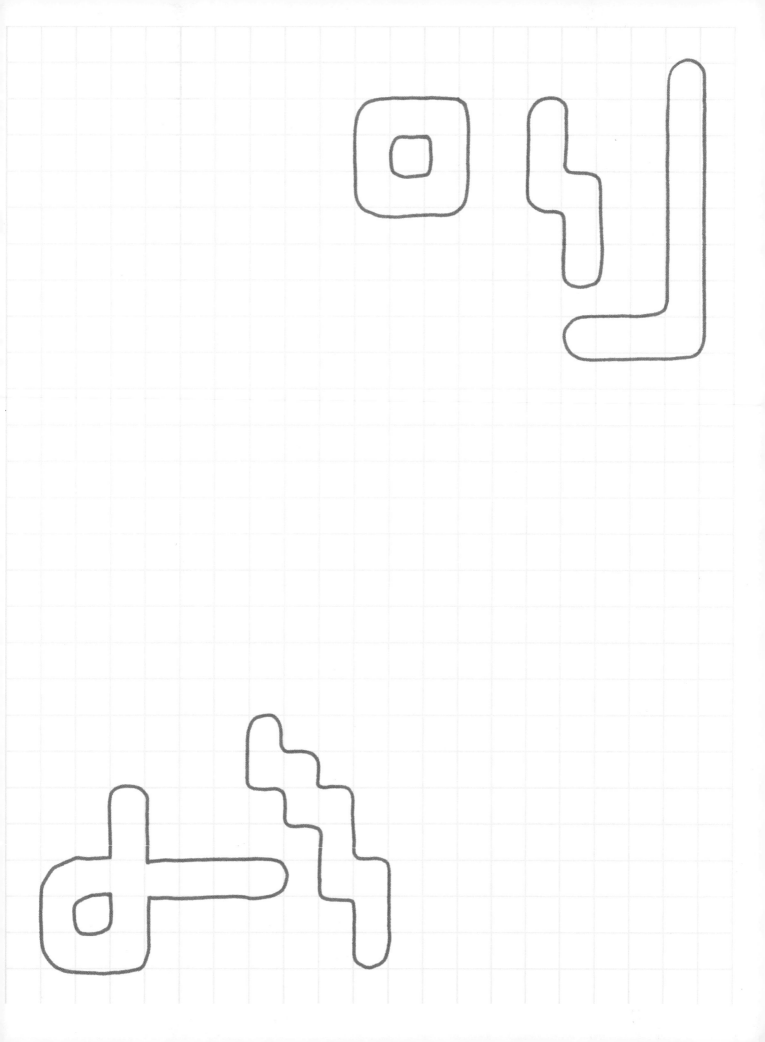

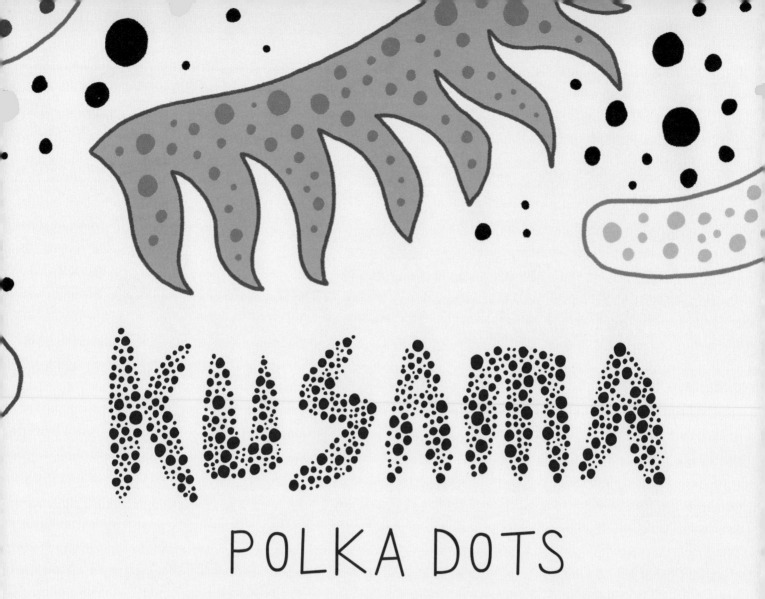

KUSAMA

POLKA DOTS

Yayoi Kusama's childhood hallucinations led to a lifelong obsession with partying polka dots, and an astounding art career spanning eight decades.

Like amoebas at a disco, Kusama's dotty designs dance with colour and energy, but there's also a dark side to this Japanese outsider's work. She once said, "I fight pain, anxiety and fear every day, and the only method I have found that relieves my illness is to keep creating art."

A champion of mental health awareness and feminism, she has consistently stood out from the crowd – just like her work.

You'll be seeing spots with this crazy combination of shape, colour and pattern.

Kusama combined dot patterns with brightly-coloured shapes.

BIG SHAPES

BLOBBY SHAPES

colours

method

1. Fill the page with big shapes and blobby shapes.

2. Use contrasting colours to fill the shapes with dots of different sizes.

3. Surround the shapes with black dots of different sizes.

tip

KEEP THE DOTS NICE AND DENSE.

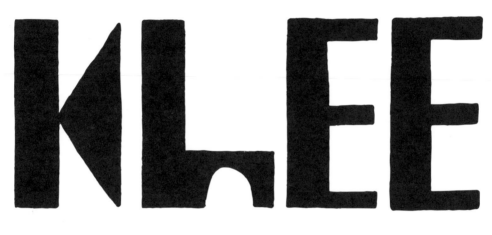

KLEE
CITYSCAPE

Paul Klee once claimed, "a drawing is simply a line going for a walk." And what incredible walks he took us on. His favoured childlike shapes might not be much to shout about on their own, but together they form intricate cityscapes, castles, boats and balloons, all dancing with colour.

Klee was an experimenter and rule-breaker, whose patchwork style transcended the schools of Expressionism, Cubism and Surrealism. His work inspired generations of artists to come, and fellow artist Robert Motherwell once called him "the supreme doodler." Who'd have thought taking a line for a walk could get you so far?

Who would have thought you could build a whole city using just a few geometric shapes?

method

1. Using the grid background as a guide, start at the bottom and fill the squares with coloured shapes.

2. Stagger the heights of the finished stacks. Once the page is about half full, add triangle rooftops and a big sun.

colours

Paul Klee created his cityscape using earthy colours and simple shapes.

shapes

3. Colour the shapes and fill in the background.

Matisse

GARDEN

For Henri Matisse, a serious illness signalled a new beginning. Already a prolific artist of the Fauvism movement, at the age of 72 he was diagnosed with cancer and confined to a wheelchair. This is when he discovered cut-out art – or, as he called it, "drawing with scissors."

Experiencing his own personal renaissance, he created vibrant collages with the aid of assistants who helped him to paint, cut out and arrange shapes on boards. By the time of his death, at age 84, he had completed arguably his most striking period, demonstrating that the simplest art can often be the most effective.

Grow your own Matisse-style garden. Fill the space opposite with loose plant shapes in a bold palette.

colours

This palette is similar to Matisse's, but you can use whatever coloured pens or pencils you have to hand.

BIG SHAPES

shapes

Matisse drew loosely, using lots of bright and pastel colours.

SMALL SHAPES

method

1. Start by drawing a few big shapes. Use a different colour for each one.

2. Fill the gaps with a variety of small shapes.

3. Fill in all of the shapes with colour.

TIMELINE

Follow the timeline of the artists and movements that feature in the book.

PABLO PICASSO

1881 – 1973

CUBIST

NATALIA GONCHAROVA

1881 – 1962

FUTURIST/RAYONIST

FERNAND LÉGER

1881 – 1955

CUBIST/PURIST

GEORGES BRAQUE

1882 – 1963

CUBIST/EXPRESSIONIST

SONIA DELAUNAY

1885 – 1979

ORPHIST

HANS ARP

1887 – 1966

DADAIST

ANDY WARHOL

1928 – 1987

POP ARTIST

FANG ZHAOLING

1914 – 2006

CALLIGRAPHIC ARTIST

LOUISE BOURGEOIS

1911 – 2010

MODERNIST/SURREALIST

MIRKA MORA

1928 – 2018

CONTEMPORARY ARTIST

YAYOI KUSAMA

1929 –

MINIMALIST/ FEMINIST ARTIST

BRIDGET RILEY

1931 –

OP ARTIST

VINCENT VAN GOGH

1853 – 1890

POST-IMPRESSIONIST

HILMA AF KLINT

1862 – 1944

ABSTRACT ARTIST

WASSILY KANDINSKY

1866 – 1944

ABSTRACT ARTIST/
EXPRESSIONIST

PAUL KLEE

1879 – 1940

EXPRESSIONIST

PIET MONDRIAN

1872 – 1944

DE STIJL/
NEO-PLASTICIST

HENRI MATISSE

1869 – 1954

FAUVIST

JOAN MIRÓ

1893 – 1983

SURREALIST

GUNTA STÖLZL

1897 – 1983

BAUHAUS

M.C. ESCHER

1898 – 1972

SURREALIST

LEE KRASNER

1908 – 1984

ABSTRACT
EXPRESSIONIST

JEAN DUBUFFET

1901 – 1985

ART BRUT/
ART INFORMEL

RENÉ MAGRITTE

1898 – 1967

SURREALIST

KEITH HARING

1958 – 1990

NEO-POP ARTIST/
STREET AND GRAFFITI
ARTIST

JEAN-MICHEL BASQUIAT

1960 – 1988

NEO-EXPRESSIONIST

TAKASHI MURAKAMI

1962 –

CONTEMPORARY
ARTIST